The Sacred Victim

ISBN: 9798863194066

Cover design by: Art Painter

Printed in France

Table of Contents

Introduction

In the annals of human history, the notion of "victim" has constantly evolved. Once silent, sometimes ignored or even ostracized, victims of various injustices now find a more central place in societal discourse. The advent of social media, the rapid evolution of human rights, and increased collective awareness have played a major role in this transformation. But in our burning desire to make up for the mistakes of the past, have we crossed a border? Have we gone from a necessary recognition to a sacralization, even a systematic heroization of the victims?

This book aims to explore this complex and nuanced phenomenon, assessing its origins, implications, and potential dangers of such a trend. This is not to deny the importance of acknowledging suffering, but to ask how we, as a society, approach this recognition.

The three parts of this book will guide the reader through an in-depth analysis of the sacralization of the victim. From its empathetic roots, through the sometimes problematic implications of heroization, to the delicate navigation between compassion and constructive criticism, each chapter offers a balanced reflection on the different aspects of this question.

By diving into "The Sacred Victim: Between Empathy and Heroic Drift," we invite the reader to take an informed and nuanced perspective, to question preconceptions, and to join us in this crucial exploration of a topic that profoundly shapes modern discourse.

Part I: Understanding the Sacralization of the Victim

At the heart of human civilizations, from its founding myths to its contemporary legends, lies one constant: storytelling. The stories we choose to tell and the stories we prefer to omit shape our collective perception of reality. Among the many protagonists who populate these stories, the figure of the victim has experienced varying fortunes. Once on the periphery, often neglected or even despised, it now seems to have migrated to the center of the stage, capturing light and sympathy. How did we get here? What are the forces that have contributed to this transformation?

The first part of this book addresses these fundamental questions. By exploring the historical and cultural origins of the sacralization of victims, we will try to discern the elements that gave rise to this phenomenon. Through this exploration, we will also examine how empathy, as a universal emotion, has been instrumental in this evolution.

Get ready for a journey through time and the human psyche, discovering the deep roots of a trend that dominates our society today. Where does our visceral need to acknowledge suffering come from? How did the repressed voices finally find an echo? These are all questions that will guide us in this first part, laying the foundation for a deeper understanding of the later sections of this book.

Definition and Origins: Tracing the historical and cultural roots of the sacralization of victims.

The notion of "victim" has come a long way throughout history, and to understand its pre-eminent place in contemporary discourse, it is necessary to examine its origins.

Definition :
At its core, a victim is a person who has suffered harm, injustice or suffering caused by others or by external circumstances. This suffering can be physical, emotional, moral or psychological. Historically, the term "victim" comes from the Latin "victima", which refers to a creature sacrificed to the gods. This origin reveals an intrinsic duality: the victim is both sacrificed and sacred.

Historical roots:

Since ancient societies, the figure of the victim has always been present. In Greco-Roman civilizations, tragedies often featured protagonists struggling with fate, victims of superior forces. Myths also abound of individuals sacrificed for the common good or to appease the gods. These stories highlight an acceptance, even expectation, of suffering and sacrifice as essential components of the human condition.

Cultural influences:
Over the centuries, different cultures and religions have shaped our perception of the victim. In Christianity, for example, Christ is both the sacrificial victim and the savior, offering a paradigm of sanctified suffering. Many other religious and philosophical traditions also incorporate notions of sacrifice, renunciation or transcended suffering.

During the modern era, with the advent of human rights movements and social revolutions, victim status began to evolve. Stories of personal suffering have taken on a political dimension, with victims becoming symbols of resistance or catalysts for change. The media, in particular, has played a crucial role in this transformation, giving voice and visibility to those who were previously marginalized.

The sacralization of victims stems from a rich structure of historical and cultural traditions. It is a complex alchemy of mythology, religion, politics and media. Understanding this genesis allows us to better understand why, today, the figure of the victim occupies such a central place in our societies.

The Empathy Floor: Why does our society feel the need to acknowledge suffering?

Empathy, the ability to feel and understand the emotions of others, is considered by many to be one of humanity's distinguishing features. It forms the foundation of our social interactions, guiding our interpersonal relationships and influencing our collective decisions. But why, as a society, do we have an almost visceral need to acknowledge the suffering of others?

Biological origins of empathy:
Science suggests that empathy has deep roots in our biology. Some researchers believe that "mirror neurons" in the brain allow us to reflect and understand the emotions of others. These neurological mechanisms would have evolved because they favored cooperation within primitive groups, a key to survival in hostile environments.

The cultural evolution of empathy:

Beyond biology, empathy has been strengthened and cultivated by cultural norms and values. Spiritual and philosophical traditions around the world have often placed compassion and care for others at the heart of their teachings. Whether it is the Christian precept "Love your neighbor as yourself" or the Buddhist notion of "universal compassion," empathy is valued and promoted as a moral ideal.

The recognition of suffering as a social binder: Acknowledging the suffering of others strengthens social bonds. This creates a sense of belonging and unity, because to recognize a person's pain is to validate their humanity. In a world where injustice is pervasive, collective recognition of suffering can also serve as a catalyst for social action and change.

The influence of the media: The modern era, with its ubiquitous media, has amplified our ability to perceive and share suffering. Poignant images and touching stories have the power to mobilize entire societies around causes. This increased visibility has reinforced our collective need to respond with empathy to stories of pain and misery.

The foundation of empathy on which our need to acknowledge suffering rests is both natural and culturally constructed. It is the expression of a deep and interconnected humanity, an innate and learned response to the pain of others. While being a powerful force for good, this collective empathy must be guided and balanced to avoid the potential pitfalls of excessive sacralization of victims.

Voices Repressed and Recognition: The Impact of the Civil Rights Movement and Social Media.

Repressed voices have long sought a way to be heard, to claim their rightful place in societal discourse. Civil rights movements and the advent of social media were two major phenomena that catalyzed this quest for recognition. Together, they have shaped our modern landscape of representation and listening.

The Civil Rights Movement: A Turning Point in the Recognition of the Marginalized

Born in the mid-20th century, the civil rights movement in the United States fought to end racial segregation and establish equal rights for all. Movement leaders, such as Martin Luther King Jr., have used civil disobedience and nonviolent protest to expose systemic injustices. The mainstream media captured these moments — black children escorted to once-white-only schools, peaceful protesters attacked by police dogs — and broadcast them to homes across the country and around the world. These images revealed the depth of suffering and evoked collective empathy, leading to profound legislative and social change.

The Advent of Social Media: The Democratization of the Voice

With the emergence of social media at the beginning of the 21st century, each individual has gained the ability to share their story with the world. Platforms like Twitter, Facebook and Instagram have become battlegrounds for human rights, social movements and justice. Hashtags such as #BlackLivesMatter or #MeToo have shed light on issues that have long been ignored or minimized. The speed at which these stories spread, the solidarity they generate, and the collective outrage they arouse have given rise to new social movements and significant changes.

The double-edged sword of recognition

While the civil rights movement and social media have played a critical role in recognizing repressed voices, this increased visibility also carries risks. Virality can sometimes lead to oversimplification of issues or a "culture of outrage" where outrage becomes the norm, drowning out more nuanced voices. Moreover, the sacralization of victims can sometimes prevent constructive and necessary criticism.

The combined impact of the civil rights movement and social media has irrevocably changed the way society recognizes and responds to repressed voices. These platforms and movements have empowered the marginalized to define their narratives and claim their rights. However, in this era of recognition, it is imperative to navigate with caution, balancing empathy and criticism, to ensure a just and balanced society.

Historical Compensation: The desire to right past mistakes and injustices.

The concept of historical compensation refers to the recognition and reparation of the harm and injustice suffered by groups of people throughout history. This desire for "reparation" stems from a collective awareness of the harm done and a desire to rectify, as far as possible, the course of events. But where does this desire come from, and how does it fit together in the current socio-political context?

Recognition of injustices

The first step towards compensation is recognition. Over time, many governments and societies have realized that certain actions or policies of the past, whether based on race, religion, gender or other factors, have caused irreparable harm. Whether slavery, colonialism, genocide or other forms of oppression, these facts, once accepted or ignored, are now widely condemned.

The moral impulse

The idea of compensation stems largely from a moral impulse. Contemporary societies, influenced by the ideals of human rights and equality, feel a responsibility towards those who have been unfairly treated in the past. This is based on an ethical conception that injustices, even historical ones, require some form of redress.

Forms of compensation

Compensation can take various forms, ranging from formal apologies to financial compensation, property or land restitution. In some cases, it may also involve the establishment of programmes or policies aimed at providing educational, economic or social opportunities for the descendants of the aggrieved persons.

Challenges and criticisms

While the intent behind historical compensation is noble, it is not without controversy. How to assess the damage suffered? How do we define who should be compensated, especially when injustices occurred generations ago? In addition, some argue that compensation can perpetuate divisions or resentments instead of promoting healing or reconciliation.

The desire to compensate for past mistakes and injustices reflects an evolution of the collective consciousness and a commitment to principles of fairness and justice. Although it is a path strewn with pitfalls and difficult questions, the quest for compensation is a testament to society's ability to self-evaluate and seek redemption for the sins of the past.

The Psychology of Empathy: Understanding our natural instincts to support and protect.

Empathy, the feeling that drives us to feel the emotions of others as if they were our own, is a fundamental feature of the human experience. It influences our interactions, guides our social behaviors and, in many cases, shapes our morality. To better understand this powerful driver of human action, let's dive into the psychology of empathy.

Biological origins of empathy

Research in neuroscience has shown that empathy has deep roots in our brains. Mirror neurons, first discovered in primates, appear to play a key role. When we observe someone else feeling an emotion or performing an action, these neurons activate as if it were our own experience, creating a bridge between ourselves and the other.

Empathy: a matter of survival:

From an evolutionary perspective, empathy may have conferred an advantage in strengthening social cohesion. In primitive societies, where survival depended on group cooperation and cohesion, those who could perceive and respond to the needs and emotions of others probably had a better chance of survival and reproduction.

Empathy and development

Empathy is not only innate; It also develops through our experiences. Children, from an early age, show signs of empathy, such as crying when another child cries. Over time, and with socialization, they learn to better understand and respond appropriately to the emotions of others.

Empathy and morality

Our ability to feel empathy influences our moral sense. Many ethical theories rely on empathy as the foundation of moral behavior, suggesting that our ability to put ourselves in the shoes of others guides us toward right and ethical actions.

Limits and dangers of empathy

Empathy, while largely beneficial, has its limits. It can make us vulnerable to manipulation or emotional exhaustion. In addition, excessive empathy can sometimes cloud our judgment, leading us to privilege the individual over the collective.

Empathy is an essential part of human psychology, shaped by evolution, biology and our life experiences. By understanding our natural instincts to support and protect, we can better navigate our relationships and build more compassionate and cohesive societies.

Part II: The Implications of Heroizing Victims

When we talk about heroes, the image that often comes to mind is that of individuals accomplishing extraordinary feats, defending just causes or overcoming insurmountable adversities. Historically, heroes were revered for their prowess, courage, and notable contributions to society. However, in today's socio-cultural landscape, a new form of heroism is emerging: the heroization of victims.

In an era marked by the sacralization of suffering, victims of injustice, trauma or misfortune are increasingly placed on a pedestal. They embody resilience in the face of adversity, bravery in vulnerability. But beyond the mere acknowledgement of their suffering, this heroization has profound implications, both positive and negative, for the individuals concerned and for society as a whole.

In this part, we will explore the ramifications of this growing trend. How does the heroization of victims influence our perception of justice, truth and morality? What are the potential benefits and dangers of this glorification? And, perhaps most crucially, how can we navigate this delicate balance between empathy and idealization, between support and sanctification?

Heroes vs. Victims: Define and distinguish two distinct concepts.

Throughout history and culture, the figures of hero and victim have occupied fundamentally different spaces in the collective narrative. While these two archetypes have overlapping areas, particularly in the contemporary world, they possess distinct characteristics that are worth exploring and defining.

1. The Hero:

Definition : Historically, a hero is a person who, in the face of adversity or from a position of weakness, shows courage, strength and sacrifices his own interests for the common good. They can be mythological figures, combatants on a battlefield, or even simple individuals displaying an extraordinary act of bravery.

Defining traits: Heroes are often characterized by bravery, resilience, determination, and ability to overcome considerable challenges.

Societal role : Heroes serve as role models. They inspire, motivate and remind members of society of what is possible to achieve or become.

2. The victim shall:

Definition : A victim is a person who has suffered harm, whether physical, emotional or psychological, usually caused by events or actions beyond his or her control.

Traits : Victims are often perceived as having been rendered powerless or vulnerable by circumstances beyond their control. Their experience is usually associated with suffering, injustice and deprivation.

Societal role : Historically, the victim has been perceived as in need of protection, support or reparation. In the modern context, recognizing someone as a victim can also mean recognizing an injustice and working to rectify it.

Areas of overlap:

In today's landscape, these two roles can sometimes mix. Victims who overcome their hardships or use their experiences to raise awareness or bring about positive change can be seen as heroes. For example, a person who has survived a serious illness and used their experience to support other patients may be considered both a victim (of the disease) and a hero (for their courage and dedication).

Although the notions of hero and victim are distinct, they are not mutually exclusive. In a society that increasingly values authenticity and resilience, the lines between these two concepts can often be blurred. However, it is essential to recognize and honor the uniqueness of each experience without falling into the trap of oversimplification or generalization.

The Prison of Victimhood: How victim status can become a permanent identity.

Recognition of suffering and injustice is essential in any society that loves justice and equity. However, when this recognition is accompanied by a prolonged fixation on victim status, it can sometimes lead to unintended consequences, transforming a temporary label into a lasting identity.

Going through a traumatic experience or being subject to injustice is undoubtedly upsetting and can leave lasting scars, both physical and emotional. Society, in its quest for solidarity and empathy, naturally tends to support those who have been wronged. However, when this support is accompanied by constant attention and reinforcement of the identity of the victim, it can have a paradoxical effect.

Instead of encouraging healing and resilience, the permanence of victim identity can lead to dependence on this role. Individuals may begin to perceive the world exclusively through the lens of their victimization, limiting their ability to evolve beyond their trauma or negative experience. This fixation on suffering can also inhibit their ability to recognize and seize opportunities, interact openly with the world, or take a more nuanced and holistic perspective on their own lives.

In addition, self-definition primarily in terms of victimization can lead to a perpetual cycle of negative expectations and biased perceptions. This can make individuals more likely to perceive affronts or injustices, even when they don't exist, reinforcing their own narrative of victimization.

It is also important to recognize that society itself plays a role in perpetuating this prison of victimization. The media, public discourse and even some well-intentioned initiatives can, unintentionally, lock individuals into this role by constantly magnifying their victimhood.

In conclusion, while recognition of suffering is vital, it is equally crucial to balance this recognition with encouragement for healing, growth and resilience. A complex, rich and multidimensional identity is the right of every individual, and it is essential to ensure that victim status does not become a chain that hinders the realization of everyone's full potential.

Dilution of Heroism: The Consequences of Confusing Suffering with Bravery.

Heroism is a concept that has historically been associated with acts of bravery, selfless gestures and sacrifices for the common good. It's a title reserved for those who exceed expectations, overcome insurmountable challenges, or put their own well-being on the line to help others. However, in our contemporary society, the definition of heroism has broadened and often confused with the simple act of enduring suffering or trauma.

When suffering alone becomes a criterion of heroism, it can lead to the dilution of the value and meaning of this concept. Not that suffering doesn't deserve recognition or empathy – it absolutely deserves it. But by systematically confusing suffering with bravery, we risk minimizing truly heroic acts that require initiative, courage and determined action.

This confusion can also create a hierarchy of suffering, where some forms of pain or trauma are considered more "heroic" than others. This can lead to unnecessary and potentially harmful comparisons between individuals, minimizing or invalidating the experiences of those who do not fit the dominant narrative of what it means to be a "hero".

Moreover, by systematically elevating victims to hero status solely on the basis of their suffering, we risk institutionalizing the victim mentality. This could encourage some people to permanently identify with their trauma or pain, potentially preventing them from pursuing healing or growth.

It is crucial to recognize and value the resilience and strength of those who have suffered. However, it is equally important to preserve the integrity of the concept of heroism, to reserve it for those who not only endure, but act, challenge and transcend, for the good of others or for a greater ideal.

Manipulations and False Victimization: The Dark Side of the Sacralization of Victims.

In a society where the recognition of victims has become paramount, a worrying phenomenon has also developed: that of false victimization. While the majority of individuals presenting themselves as victims are sincere in their testimonies, there is unfortunately a minority that exploits collective compassion for a variety of reasons, often selfish. This behaviour stems in part from the sacralization of victims, where mere identification as such can provide attention, support or various benefits.

False victimization takes on many faces. It can arise in public debates, where some, wanting to win sympathy or direct opinion to their advantage, wave a false banner of victimization. It can also appear in more personal contexts, where individuals seek to manipulate those around them for compassion, support, or even material benefits.

This phenomenon is not without consequences. Every instance of false victimization undermines the credibility of the real victims. It creates skepticism that may, in the long run, make society less inclined to believe or support those who have actually been harmed. Moreover, it diverts attention and resources from real victims, who may desperately need them.

Manipulation through false victimization can also have serious legal or societal consequences. False accusations can ruin lives, destroy reputations and distort the judicial process. Moreover, by propagating a narrative of victimization, false testimony can further polarize debates, make the search for truth more difficult, and sow discord within communities.

It is therefore crucial for society to approach this topic with great caution and an acute awareness of the nuances. While continuing to support genuine victims and fight injustices, it is essential to cultivate critical thinking, encourage thorough investigations and promote the truth. In a world where the sincerity of suffering should be self-evident, it is tragic but necessary to remain vigilant against those who might fake it for dishonest purposes.

Societal Manichaeism: The tendency to divide the world into good guys and bad guys.

Complexity and nuance are often the first victims in a deeply polarized society. At the heart of this polarization lies a Manichean perspective, a worldview that divides humanity into two distinct camps: the "good guys" and the "bad guys." This simplistic prism, while attractive in its clarity, is fertile ground for misunderstandings, conflicts and misunderstandings.

History is replete with examples where Manichaeism has guided perception and politics. Whether during religious wars, the Cold War or in contemporary conflicts, this tendency to see the world in terms of black and white has proven to be a human constant. However, the speed and ubiquity of social media has amplified this phenomenon, making nuance an increasingly scarce commodity.

What makes Manichaeism particularly worrying is its ability to dehumanize. When individuals or groups are viewed solely through the prism of right or wrong, their intrinsic complexity is ignored. Their motivations, fears, hopes and dreams are relegated to the background, replaced by stereotypes and prejudices. In this context, mutual understanding and dialogue become almost impossible, because each side is convinced of the absolute rightness of its cause and the malignancy of the opposition.

In addition, Manichaeism feeds a culture of blame. Instead of seeking collaborative solutions, society finds itself trapped in cycles of blame and recrimination. Responsibility is constantly outsourced, with each side blaming the other for all the ills. In this climate, mistakes are never admitted, and learning becomes difficult, if not impossible.

In the face of these challenges, it is imperative to cultivate nuance, curiosity and open-mindedness. It is vital to recognize that reality is often far more complex than simplistic dichotomies of right and wrong. Each individual, each culture, each nation has its own history, its own challenges and its own aspirations. By embracing this complexity, society can hope to break out of the traps of Manichaeism and move towards a deeper and more authentic understanding of the human condition.

Part III: Navigating Between Compassion and Constructive Criticism

In tumultuous times marked by rapid social change, global challenges and increasing polarization, society's ability to address issues with both compassion and constructive criticism is more crucial than ever. If, on the one hand, empathy and solidarity are essential to create a strong and resilient social fabric, on the other, healthy critical thinking is necessary to avoid the pitfalls of dogmatism, Manichaeism and manipulation.

Skilfully navigating between these two poles can seem like a daunting task. Compassion, often emotional and visceral, may seem at odds with the more rational and detached nature of criticism. Yet these two forces are not mutually exclusive. On the contrary, they can and must coexist for a society to thrive, learn and adapt.

In this part, we will explore the delicate alchemy between compassion and constructive criticism. We will examine how individuals and communities can balance their natural desire to support and protect with the imperative need to question, analyze and, where appropriate, challenge. Ultimately, our goal is to chart a course that respects both heart and mind, recognizing that it is in this balance that lies the true potential of an enlightened and progressive society.

The Importance of Nuance: Why a balanced approach is essential.

In the tumult of contemporary social, political and cultural debates, nuance is often the first victim. Carried away by waves of emotion, passion and sometimes dogmatism, we are tempted to simplify problems, to reduce them to easy dichotomies, thus depriving discussions of their richness and complexity. Yet it is precisely this nuance that is the foundation of genuine understanding and real progress.

A balanced approach reminds us that few situations can be fully categorized in terms of black and white. The most pressing issues of our time, be they climate change, social inequality, human rights or technology, are profoundly complex. They require an appreciation of nuances, details and different perspectives to be fully understood.

Ignoring these subtleties can have serious consequences. This can lead to ill-adapted solutions, misunderstandings and unnecessary conflicts. In addition, an oversimplified worldview risks making us impervious to learning and adaptation, because it leaves no room for questioning, curiosity or discovery.

Embracing nuance, on the other hand, enriches the public debate. It fosters empathy because it forces us to recognize the validity of perspectives other than our own. It also encourages innovation, because by exploring the different facets of a problem, we are more likely to discover original and effective solutions.

Ultimately, a balanced and nuanced approach is essential not only for our collective understanding of the challenges we face, but also for our ability to respond judiciously. By valuing nuance, we give ourselves the means to move forward with discernment, wisdom and inclusiveness, essential traits for a society that aspires to an enlightened and harmonious future.

Responsible Media: The role of the media in representing victims.

The media, in their various forms, have always played a crucial role in shaping public opinion and constructing social realities. In the context of victim representation, their responsibility is all the more important. They shape, often unconsciously, our perception of events, the individuals involved, and broader contexts.

First, how the media chooses to portray victims has profound implications. Meaningful and empathetic media coverage can draw attention to injustices, raise awareness of issues that are often ignored, and give a voice to those who are marginalized. However, sensationalist or biased coverage can distort reality, perpetuate harmful stereotypes and even revictimize those already suffering.

The issue of media accountability also extends to fact-checking. In a world saturated with information and where fake news can spread like wildfire, it is imperative that the media maintain high standards of accuracy and integrity. Presenting unverified or ill-informed narratives can not only mislead the public, but also cause irreparable harm to individuals or communities.

In addition, the media must carefully navigate between the privacy of victims and the public's right to information. Too often, in the race for scoops or under the pressure of competition, the limits are crossed, jeopardizing the dignity and well-being of the people concerned.

Faced with these issues, it is crucial that the media take a thoughtful, balanced and ethical approach when dealing with topics involving victims. This requires ongoing training, self-reflection and, sometimes, questioning established practices. Codes of ethics and editorial standards need to be regularly reviewed and adapted to changing contexts and sensitivities.

In conclusion, while the media have the power to inform, educate and raise awareness, they also bear a heavy responsibility. By addressing the issue of victims with integrity, empathy and accuracy, they can contribute meaningfully to a more just, enlightened and compassionate society.

Education and Awareness: Cultivating a conscious and thoughtful society.

Education is one of the most powerful pillars on which a society can be built. It shapes minds, guides behaviours and determines, in large part, the future trajectory of a community or nation. In an ever-changing world, marked by increasing complexities and unprecedented challenges, the importance of education and awareness cannot be underestimated.

Education is not only about acquiring academic knowledge; It also encompasses character training, inculcation of values and development of critical thinking. A well-designed education can equip individuals with the tools to decipher the world around them, to ask relevant questions and to consider innovative solutions.

Awareness, on the other hand, is the process by which individuals become aware of issues, realities and challenges that may otherwise remain invisible or misunderstood. It plays a crucial role in highlighting injustices, fostering empathy and mobilizing collectively around important causes.

In the context of victim representation, for example, education and awareness are essential. Informing younger generations about the stories, contexts and challenges faced by different communities or individuals can encourage greater empathy, understanding and a deeper commitment to justice and equity. In addition, by cultivating critical thinking, individuals are better prepared to identify biases, challenge stereotypes and engage in constructive debate.

However, for education and awareness to be effective, they must be constantly renewed and adapted. As new challenges emerge and societies evolve, educational programs and outreach initiatives must reflect these changes, ensuring their relevance and impact.

Ultimately, a conscious and reflective society is one that recognizes the intrinsic worth of each individual, fights injustice, and constantly strives to better understand and improve the world around them. By investing in education and awareness, we are laying the foundation for a brighter, more inclusive and harmonious future.

Complex Stories: Accepting and understanding individual stories in all their complexity.

Each individual is a sum of multiple experiences, influences, dreams, trials and aspirations. Yet in the whirlwind of our modern world, these individual stories, rich and nuanced, are often simplified to reductive narratives, even stereotypes. These simplifications, while sometimes practical for media storytelling or social categorization, often unfairly ignore the real complexity of human life.

Accepting and understanding individual stories in all their complexity is not only a matter of humanity, it is also an imperative for a society that aims to be inclusive, equitable and empathetic. By recognizing the depth and diversity of human experiences, we offer essential dignity and facilitate mutual understanding.

It's easy to fall into the trap of generalizations, especially in an age where information is quickly consumed and shared. However, behind every stat, catchy headline, and general trend, there are people with unique stories. Some of these stories can be uplifting, some tragic, some inspiring, some confusing. But all deserve to be heard and understood.

This recognition is particularly relevant in the context of victim representation. Too often, victims are portrayed in a monolithic pattern, obscuring the different facets of their identity, the unique circumstances of their situation or even the nuances of their experiences. By focusing on a single dimension of their history, we risk not only dehumanizing them, but also failing to grasp the breadth and specificity of their experience.

This is why it is essential to cultivate an approach that values complexity. Whether in the media, schools, or public discussions, efforts must be made to ensure that individual narratives are not overshadowed by generalities. Spaces must be created to allow these stories to be revealed, nuanced, and ultimately, understood in all their richness.

In an increasingly polarized society, where divisions seem to be deepening, such an approach is a lifeline. By embracing the complexity of individual stories, we build bonds of understanding, build bridges of empathy, and strengthen the social fabric that unites humanity in its splendid diversity.

Restorative Justice: Focus on healing rather than mere recognition.

The notion of justice is intrinsic to the very structure of our societies. It serves as the foundation of our legal systems, moral values and collective aspirations. Traditionally, justice is often seen as a mechanism of punishment or retribution. However, there is another, less punitive but more restorative perspective that is gaining ground and redefining the way we think about justice: restorative justice.

Restorative justice is distinguished by its approach to healing and restoration. Rather than focusing solely on punishing the culprit, it aims to repair the damage done, restore broken relationships, and promote holistic healing for all parties involved. She recognizes that behind every wrongdoing are complex stories, emotions, and dynamics that require deep attention and understanding.

In the context of the sacralization of victims, restorative justice offers an alternative path. Instead of simply acknowledging the suffering or harm suffered, it looks at concrete ways to promote healing and reconciliation. This may include discussions between the victim and the perpetrator, community mediations or reparations programmes.

This approach in no way minimizes the seriousness of the act committed or the suffering of the victim. On the contrary, it seeks to offer a space where this suffering can be expressed, understood and ultimately appeased. It recognizes that isolation or stigmatization of the perpetrator may not always be beneficial in the long run and that there are alternative pathways that can lead to true redemption and positive transformation.

However, the implementation of restorative justice requires a profound questioning of our traditional systems and mindsets. It requires a collective will to move beyond punitive impulses and seek solutions that truly promote healing, understanding and peace.

Ultimately, restorative justice reminds us that justice, in its purest essence, should seek not only to punish, but also to heal, restore and reunite. In a world where divisions and wounds seem to be deepening, this approach offers a glimmer of hope and a model for building more resilient, empathetic and cohesive communities.

Avoiding Politicization of Victims: The Need to Keep Victims' Stories Out of the Political Arena.

In the modern world, where every event, story and injustice can be immediately amplified by the media and social networks, there is a growing risk that individuals or groups will be instrumentalized for political ends. The victims, often at the heart of heated and passionate debates, are not immune to this dynamic. The politicization of victims, that is, the use of their history or suffering for political purposes, can distort their experience, further polarize society and ultimately harm the cause they embody.

First, instrumentalizing victims for specific political agendas can lead to an oversimplification of their histories. In the need to tailor a narrative to a cause or campaign, individual nuances, complexities, and specifics may be omitted. This process can not only distort public perception, but also alienate the victims themselves, who may feel misunderstood or manipulated.

Moreover, when victims' stories are captured and amplified in the political arena, they often become pawns in power games, reducing their humanity and experience to mere rhetorical tools. In such contexts, the real issue – justice, healing or change – can be overshadowed by partisan battles.

The politicization of victims can also polarize society. Rather than encouraging constructive dialogue or collective empathy, it can deepen divisions, fuelling a climate of hostility and mistrust. In such scenarios, instead of bringing people together around a common cause, the stories of victims may unintentionally drive them apart.

It is therefore essential to treat victims' stories with respect, integrity and sensitivity. Keeping these stories out of the political arena does not mean that they should not influence necessary policies or reforms. On the contrary, it simply means that their use should never be opportunistic or reductive. Their voices deserve to be heard for what they are: authentic testimonies of suffering, resilience and humanity.

In an era where truth is sometimes elastic and manipulation is commonplace, it is all the more important to anchor our public debates in an ethic of respect and authenticity. By avoiding the politicization of victims, we honour their experiences and strengthen the quality and integrity of public discourse.

The Path to Resilience: Encouraging victims to find their inner strength.

Resilience is that mysterious yet essential ability of the human soul to overcome adversity, to rise after a fall, to find light even in the darkest moments. For those who have been victims, whether of injustice, trauma, or violence, the road to resilience can seem arduous, even insurmountable. Yet it is precisely in these deep valleys of suffering that many people discover an unsuspected inner strength.

Encouraging victims to find and nurture this strength is not a simple task. This requires deep understanding, sincere empathy and constant accompaniment. Here are some key steps on this path to resilience:

1. Recognition and Validation: The first step towards healing is often recognition. Victims need to feel heard, understood and validated in their feelings and experiences. A simple act of active listening can be incredibly therapeutic.

2. Security and Stability: Before victims can heal, it is essential that victims feel safe, both physically and emotionally. This may require professional interventions, support networks or environmental changes.

3. Expression and Catharsis: Finding ways to express pain, whether through art, speech, music, or other forms of creativity, can help victims process and release their restrained emotions.

4. Reaffirmation of Identity: It is crucial that victims do not define themselves solely by their trauma. Activities that build self-esteem, confidence, and personal identity can help rediscover who they are outside of their traumatic experience.

5. Community Connection: Being surrounded by a support network – whether it's support groups, friends, family, or mentors – can provide an emotional safety net and strengthen a sense of belonging.

6. Vision for the Future: Focusing on future goals, dreams and aspirations can help redirect victims' attention to a positive and promising future.

7. Empowerment: Finally, encouraging victims to regain control of their lives, make strong choices, and feel in control of their destiny can transform their sense of powerlessness into restored power.

Encouraging resilience does not mean minimizing suffering or ignoring the severity of trauma. Rather, it recognizes that even in the midst of the deepest pain there is potential for healing, growth, and rebirth. By supporting victims on this path, we celebrate the tremendous capacity of the human being to transcend his trials and to find, even in scars, signs of magnificent inner strength.

Criticize without Blame: The distinction between questioning a narrative and blaming the victim.

In contemporary society, where discourses are often polarized and the stakes are highly sensitive, it is vital to navigate with caution and discernment. A particularly tricky area is the ability to criticize or question a narrative without falling into the trap of victim-blame. This requires a nuanced understanding of the distinction between these two actions and a clear intention to approach the situation with empathy and respect.

To criticize a narrative is to evaluate or analyze a story or statement to understand its validity, coherence or authenticity. It is an intellectual exercise that seeks to distinguish truth from fiction, or to understand the motivations and circumstances surrounding a particular event. In some cases, this may involve asking tough questions, looking for evidence, or questioning apparent inconsistencies. It is a process that, when conducted with integrity, aims to enlighten, understand and inform.

On the other hand, blaming the victim is an act of judgment that attributes the fault or responsibility for the traumatic event to the victim himself. This goes beyond simply questioning a narrative, as it involves moral condemnation, often based on prejudices, stereotypes or ignorance of the facts. Blaming the victim can have devastating consequences, as it minimizes or delegitimizes their experience, retraumatizes them, and perpetuates cycles of shame and silence.

It is therefore crucial to navigate carefully between these two poles. This involves actively listening, asking questions sensitively, and refraining from jumping to conclusions. It also requires an awareness of our own biases and a willingness to approach each situation with an open and empathetic mindset.

In an age of fake news, deep divisions, and societal challenges, it is all the more important to seek the truth carefully, while avoiding further harm to those who have already been hurt. With discernment and compassion, we can hope to build a more just and understanding society, where every voice is heard and every experience is respected.

The Art of Active Listening: Giving room for diverse and varied voices.

In an age saturated with noise, strong opinions and continuous information, the art of active listening has become an essential, even vital, skill. It is not only about perceiving the words spoken, but also about understanding the intention, context and emotion behind them. Active listening is the key to giving space to diverse and varied voices, allowing for deep understanding and authentic exchange.

Active listening is not just about hearing; It requires total presence, conscious commitment and an empathetic response. It is a posture that involves putting aside one's own prejudices, opinions, and distractions to fully immerse oneself in the other's experience. This requires asking relevant questions, reflecting what has been said, and validating each other's feelings.

In the context of our diverse societies, where voices from different backgrounds, cultures, experiences and perspectives seek to be heard, active listening becomes a powerful tool for building bridges of understanding. It recognizes and values individuality, while emphasizing our common humanity. It encourages dialogue rather than debate, connection rather than confrontation.

Giving space to diverse and varied voices enriches our collective perspective, broadens our field of understanding and strengthens the social fabric. However, for these voices to be truly heard, they must be received with respect, openness and kindness. Active listening, in this sense, is not only a skill, but a responsibility, a way of honoring the dignity and worth of each individual.

By cultivating the art of active listening, we choose to engage in a world where every story counts, every voice has its place, and where the diversity of human experiences is celebrated and cherished. It is an invitation to evolve beyond the mere echoes of our own opinions to embrace the richness and complexity of the human chorus in all its glory.

Conclusion and Way Forward: Summary of Key Lessons and Steps for a Balanced Society.

Through our exploration of the nuances inherent in victim recognition, constructive criticism, and the importance of listening, we have uncovered a myriad of challenges and opportunities that shape our society today. Every voice, every story, every individual experience is a unique thread in the complex fabric of our collective coexistence.

The key lessons we can draw are multiple:

1. Recognition Without Idolatry: While validating and honoring the experiences of victims, it is essential to avoid locking them into a one-dimensional identity, thereby allowing for growth, healing, and evolution.

2. Critique with Empathy: The ability to question, analyze and criticize is fundamental to a healthy society. However, this must be done with sensitivity, avoiding blame and judgment.

3. Active listening as a foundation: True listening transcends mere hearing. It builds bridges, strengthens connections and encourages authentic dialogue, which is essential for a vibrant and inclusive society.

In considering a way forward, we must commit to:

- **Educate and Raise Awareness:** Be proactive in educating youth and adults about the nuances of storytelling, compassion, and the importance of listening.

- **Promote Responsible Media:** Encourage balanced media representation, avoiding sensationalization and favoring depth and nuance.

- **Cultivate Resilience:** Provide the tools and resources to help individuals overcome adversity, heal and transform.

- **Engage in Continuous Dialogue:** Foster forums, debates and spaces where people can exchange ideas, share experiences and learn from each other.

A balanced society will not be free from conflict or disagreement. However, by cultivating a culture of empathy, mutual respect and open-mindedness, we will be able to navigate through these challenges with a clear vision and a collective will to move towards a harmonious future. A society where every voice counts, where every individual is valued, and where we, together, write a story that celebrates not only our differences, but also our shared humanity.

www.ingramcontent.com/pod-product-compliance
Lightning Source LLC
Chambersburg PA
CBHW050851260726

48660CB00006B/2574